YOUR KNOWLEDGE HAS VALUE

Bibliographic information published by the German National Library:

The German National Library lists this publication in the National Bibliography; detailed bibliographic data are available on the Internet at http://dnb.dnb.de .

Imprint:

Copyright © 2015 GRIN Verlag, Open Publishing GmbH
Print and binding: Books on Demand GmbH, Norderstedt Germany
ISBN: 978-3-668-10588-1

This book at GRIN:

http://www.grin.com/en/e-book/310580/single-and-multiple-target-tracking

Mohamed El-Ghoboushi

Single and multiple target tracking

GRIN Publishing

GRIN - Your knowledge has value

Since its foundation in 1998, GRIN has specialized in publishing academic texts by students, college teachers and other academics as e-book and printed book. The website www.grin.com is an ideal platform for presenting term papers, final papers, scientific essays, dissertations and specialist books.

Visit us on the internet:

http://www.grin.com/

http://www.facebook.com/grincom

http://www.twitter.com/grin_com

Target Tracking

Prepared by

Eng. Mohamed El-Ghoboushi

October, 2015

Contents

- Introduction
- New topics in target tracking
- Overview of object tracking
- Target tracking

What is tracking?

• Tracking can be defined as the problem of approximating the path of an object in the object plane.

Introduction

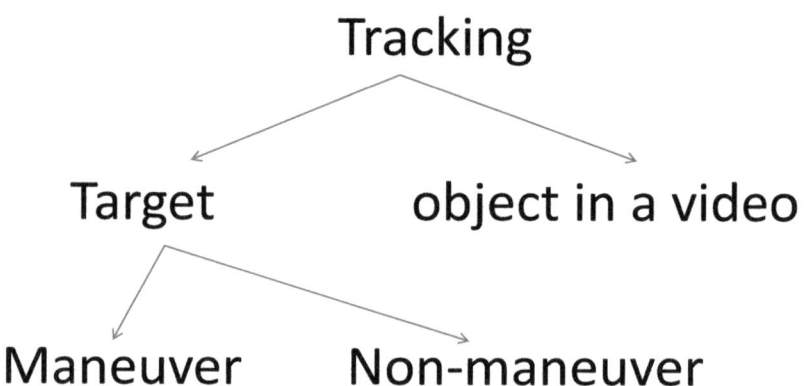

Introduction

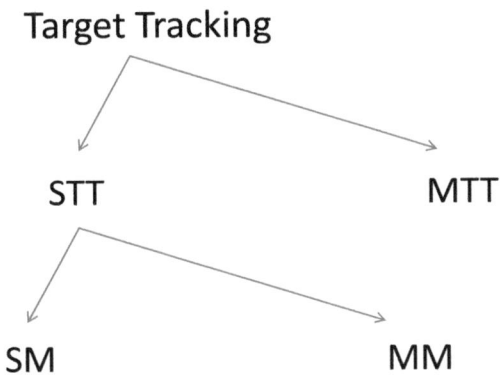

Target Tracking

STT   MTT

SM   MM

What are the new topics in target tracking?

- Target Tracking in Wireless Sensor Network
- Multiple Target Localization Using Compressive Sensing
- **Real-time visual tracking using compressive sensing**

Target Tracking in Wireless Sensor Network

- Target tracking is concerned with approximating the trajectory of one or more moving objects based on some partial information, usually provided by sensors .

- Target tracking protocols can be mainly classified into five schemes, **which are**: tree-based tracking, cluster-based tracking, prediction-based tracking, mobicast message-based tracking and hybrid methods

Target Tracking in Wireless Sensor Network

- Sensor networks used in target tracking face two kinds of major problems: efficient networking & energy-saving techniques (as sensors have to communicate with one another or with a base to transmit results of local computation) and efficient processing of information gathered by sensors.

OPEN RESEARCH ISSUES

- application of WSN in a variety of application areas brought many open issues to researchers.

Open research issues for target tracking applications _include_:

o Dealing with moving object direction changes and varying speeds.

o Energy efficient missing target track recovery

OPEN RESEARCH ISSUES

- Performance comparison of static and dynamic network
- Relationship between energy consumption with cluster formation
- Tracking Precision & Prediction Accuracy.
- Designing well organized computing and nominal transmission of messages without degradation of performance as message transmission consumes a lot of energy
- Sensor node fault tolerance

Overview

of

Object Tracking

What is Object tracking?

- The aim of *object tracking* is to *find an object of a pre-defined class in a video frame.*

- Video structures consists of *multiple frames.*

- Three stages of data treating: object extraction, object recognition and tracking, and decisions about activities.

Basic steps for tracking an object

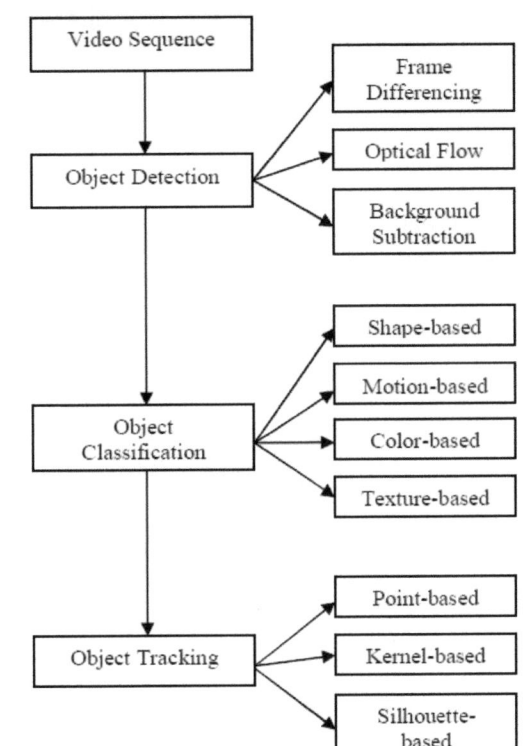

Video Sequence

↓

Object Detection
→ Frame Differencing
→ Optical Flow
→ Background Subtraction

↓

Object Classification
→ Shape-based
→ Motion-based
→ Color-based
→ Texture-based

↓

Object Tracking
→ Point-based
→ Kernel-based
→ Silhouette-based

Object Represention

Object representations. (a) Centroid, (b) multiple points, (c) rectangular patch, (d) elliptical patch, (e) part-based multiple patches, (f) object skeleton, (g) control points on object contour, (h) complete object contour, (i) object silhouette

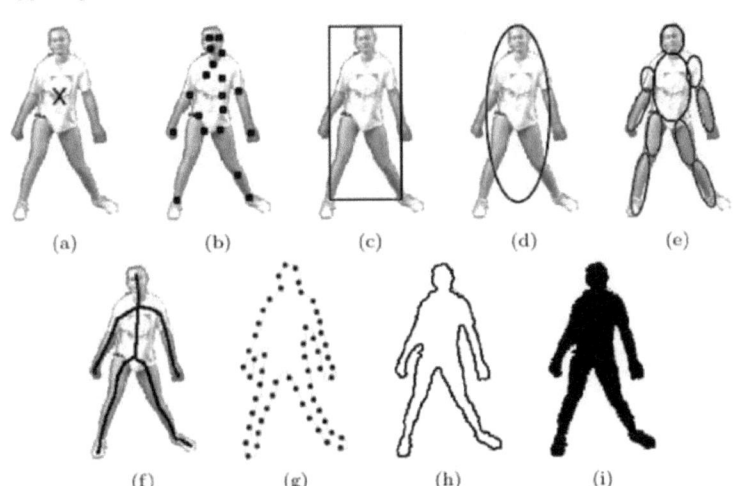

(a)   (b)   (c)   (d)   (e)

(f)   (g)   (h)   (i)

Object Represention

Appearance representations:

- Templates. Formed using simple geometric shapes or silhouettes. Suitable for tracking objects whose poses do not vary considerably during the course of tracking. Self-adapation of templates during the tracking is possibe.

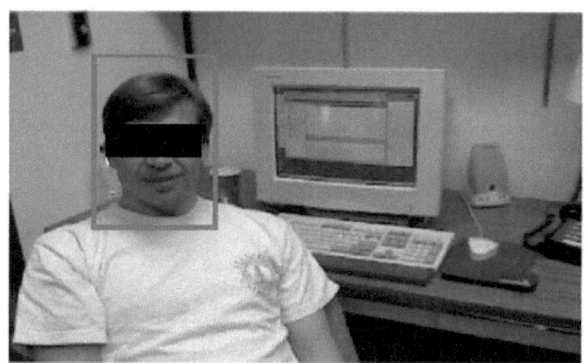

http://signal.ee.psu.edu/Behavior_Recognition.pdf

References

[1] J.Joshan Athanesious, P.Suresh, "Systematic Survey on Object Tracking Methods in Video", International Journal of Advanced Research in Computer Engineering & Technology (IJARCET) Volume 1, Issue 8, October 2012.

[2] Himani S. Parekh, Darshak G. Thakore, Udesang K. Jaliya , "A Survey on Object Detection and Tracking Methods", International Journal of Innovative Research in Computer and Communication Engineering An ISO 3297: 2007 Certified Organization) Vol. 2, Issue 2, February 2014

[3] G.Mallikarjuna Rao, Dr. Ch.Satyanarayana, " Visual Object Target Tracking Using Particle Filter: A Survey", I.J. Image, Graphics and Signal Processing, 2013, 6, 57-71

[4] Alper Yilmaz, Omar Javed, Mubarak Shah, " Object Tracking: A Survey", ACM Computing Surveys, Vol. 38, No. 4, Article 13, Publication date: December 2006.

Contents

- Introduction
- Overview of object tracking
- Target tracking

What is target tracking?

- The key to successful target tracking lies in the optimal extraction of useful information about the target's state from the observations.

- A good model of the target will certainly facilitate this information extraction to a great extent.

Maneuver and *Non-maneuver Target*

- Target motions are normally classified into *two* classes of modes: *maneuver* and *non-maneuver*.

- A *non-maneuvering motion* is the *straight and level motion* at a constant velocity, sometimes also referred to as the *uniform motion*.

- All the other motions belong to the maneuvering mode

Target motion modeling

- Target motion modeling is one of the first tasks for maneuvering target tracking.

- It aims at developing a model that well accounts for the effect of target motion and is easily tractable.

- We will try to describe the efforts and results in modeling the target motion for tracking a maneuvering target without knowing its true dynamic behaviors.

Target motion modeling

These *efforts* have been made along <u>two lines</u>:

- Approximate the actually nonrandom control input u_k as a random process of certain properties.
- Describe typical target trajectories by some representative motion models with properly designed parameters.

The State Space Model

- Both good models to describe the target dynamics and sensor will certainly help the information extraction.
- Most of the tracking algorithms base their performance on the a *priori* defined *mathematical model* of the target which is assumed to be sufficiently accurately.
- The first challenge is the problem of describing the target motion model and establishes a good compromise between accuracy and complexity.

The Dynamic System Model

- *System Equation:*

$$x_k = f_k\left(x_{k-1}, u_{k-1}^s, v_{k-1}\right)$$

x_k : target state vector, $\qquad$ u_k^s : system input vector

v_k : system noise sequence with covariance matrix $\quad Q_k^s$

f_k : vector-valued state-transition function (possibly non-linear)

- *Measurement Equation:*

$$y_k = h_k\left(x_k, u_k^m, w_k\right)$$

y_k : measurement vector, $\qquad$ u_k^m : measurement input vector

w_k : measurement noise sequence with covariance matrix $\quad Q_k^m$

h_k : vector-valued measurement function (possibly non-linear)

Mode versus Model

The terms target mode and target model are used to address *two* different realities:

- The *target mode* refers to the true target behavior or target motion.

- The *target model* is a mathematical model usually contains simplified description of the of the target motion with a certain accuracy level.

- The primary *objective* of target tracking is to *estimate the state trajectories of a target* (a moving object).

- Although a target is almost *never* really a point in the space and the information about its orientation is valuable for tracking, a target is usually treated as a point object without a shape in tracking, especially in target dynamic models.

- A *target dynamic model* or motion model describes the evolution of the target state x with respect to time.

- Almost all maneuvering target tracking methods are model-based.

- They assume that the target motion and its observations can be represented by some known mathematical models accurately.

- The most commonly used such models are those known as **state-space models**

Continuous   **Discrete**   **Hybrid**

- *The* **continuous-time** *model:*

$$\dot{x}(t) = A(t)x(t) + D(t)u(t) + B(t)w(t); \quad x(t_0) = x_0$$
$$z(t) = C(t)x(t) + v(t)$$

Where A(t), D(t), B(t) and C(t) are the continuous-time and w(t) and v(t) are the continuous-time process and measurement noise with covariances Q(t) and R(t), respectively.

The discrete-time model:

- The state equation:

$$x_{k+1} = F_k x_k + G_k u_k + E_k w_k$$

- The measurement equation:

$$z_k = H_k x_k + v_k$$

Where:

$$F_k = F(t_{k+1}, t_k) = F(t_{k+1} - t_k) = F(\Delta t) = e^{A\Delta t}$$

$$G_k \triangleq G(t_{k+1}, t_k) = \int_0^{\Delta t} e^{A(\Delta t - \tau)} D d\tau.$$

The discrete-time model (cont.):

The process noise $w(t)$ is considered to be zero-mean and white Gaussian. The discretized process noise w_k retains the same characteristics

$$E[w_k] = 0, \quad E[w_k w_j'] = Q_k \delta_{kj}$$

With covariance Q_k given by

$$Q_k = \int_0^{\Delta t} e^{A(\Delta t - \tau)} BQB' e^{A'(\Delta t - \tau)} d\tau.$$

The mixed-time model (Hybrid):

- Since the *observations* are usually only available at discrete time instants and the target motion is more accurately modeled by the continuous time equation, it is more appropriate to use the following continuous-discrete time form:

$$\dot{x}(t) = A(t)x(t) + D(t)u(t) + B(t)w(t); \quad x(t_0) = x_0$$

$$z_k = H_k x_k + v_k$$

- Let The target is assumed to have a 2D horizontal motion model with a state described by

$$x = \begin{bmatrix} x & \dot{x} & y & \dot{y} \end{bmatrix}'$$

Where (x,y) is the target position in Cartesian coordinates and $\dot{x}$ and $\dot{y}$ are the linear velocity of the target along the x-axis and the y-axis, respectively

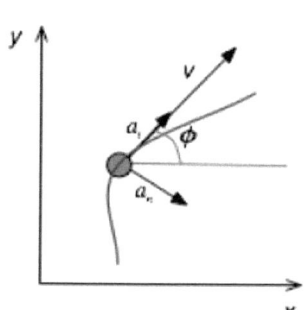

- The target dynamics are described by:

$$\begin{cases} \dot{x}(t) = v(t) \cos \phi(t) \\ \dot{y}(t) = v(t) \sin \phi(t) \\ \dot{v}(t) = a_t(t) \\ \dot{\phi}(t) = a_n(t)/v(t) \end{cases}$$

- Where v and ϕ are the linear velocity and (velocity) heading angle, respectively. The variables a_t and a_n are the target tangential and normal accelerations in the horizontal plane, respectively.

This model can explain several target motions including the **special cases**:

- Rectilinear, *constant velocity* motion
$$(a_n = 0, a_t = 0)$$

- Rectilinear, *accelerated motion*
$$(a_n = 0, a_t \neq 0)$$

- Circular, *constant speed motion*
$$(a_n \neq 0, a_t = 0)$$

Non-maneuver Target Dynamic Models
Constant-Velocity (CV) models $(a_n = 0, a_t = 0)$

In a two-dimensional scenario where the altitude z is not considered, the model takes the more popular form, the target state vector is given by

$$\dot{x}(t) = A_{CV}x(t) + B_{CV}w(t)$$

$$A_{CV} = \begin{bmatrix} 0 & 1 & 0 & 0 \\ 0 & 0 & 0 & 0 \\ 0 & 0 & 0 & 1 \\ 0 & 0 & 0 & 0 \end{bmatrix}, \quad B_{CV} = \begin{bmatrix} 0 & 0 \\ 1 & 0 \\ 0 & 0 \\ 0 & 1 \end{bmatrix}$$

Where $w(t)$ is white Gaussian noise with covariance,

$$E[w(t)w(\tau)'] = Q(t)\delta(t - \tau) \quad \& \quad Q(t) = \text{diag}(\sigma_x^2, \sigma_y^2).$$

The discrete-time equivalent of the above model is described by $x_{k+1} = F_{cv}x_k + G_{cv}w_k$

The discrete-time transition matrix is given by

$$F_{CV} = \begin{bmatrix} 1 & \Delta t & 0 & 0 \\ 0 & 1 & 0 & 0 \\ 0 & 0 & 1 & \Delta t \\ 0 & 0 & 0 & 1 \end{bmatrix}.$$

Note that the *control input* $u = 0$ in the **non-maneuvering** models.

Mathematical Model for Sensory System

- As the problem of target tracking is that it is essential to extract the most information about the target state from the observations, thus besides modeling the target; it is also necessary to model the sensor.

- The **sensor** described is RADAR and is considered to be placed at the origin of the Cartesian axis, i.e., is placed in the coordinates $(x, y) = (0, 0)$, and the sensor coordinate system is polar providing in each measurement the range r and the bearing θ of the target

- The sensor measurements are modeled with the following additive noise:

$$r = \bar{r} + v_r$$

$$\theta = \bar{\theta} + v_\theta$$

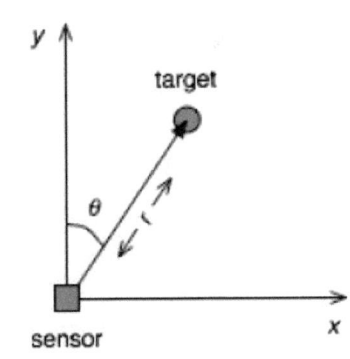

- Where $x_k^p = (\bar{r}, \bar{\theta})$ is the nominal target position, in the sensor polar coordinates and $v_k^p = (v_r, v_\theta)$ are the respective measurement errors, assumed to be zero-mean, Gaussian distributed and uncorrelated.

Mathematical Model for Sensory System

- Considering the measurement error vector in polar coordinates at the time step k

$$v_k^p \sim \mathcal{N}(0, R_k^p)$$

$$R_k^p = \text{cov}(v_k^p) = \text{diag}(\sigma_r^2, \sigma_\theta^2) = R^p \quad \forall k.$$

- The sensor measurements in the sensor coordinate system is given by

$$z_k^p = \begin{bmatrix} r \\ \theta \end{bmatrix} = h(x_k) + v_k^p$$

- Where the error-free position of the target in polar coordinates is given by

$$x_k^c = h(x_k) = \begin{bmatrix} \bar{r}_k \\ \bar{\theta}_k \end{bmatrix} = \begin{bmatrix} \sqrt{x_k^2 + y_k^2} \\ f(y_k, x_k) \end{bmatrix}$$

Maneuver Detection

- Many maneuvering target tracking techniques require a method for detecting the maneuver before compensation of the state estimate can be accomplished.
- This is the case in approaches which use a "quiescent" constant-velocity model such as the variable-dimension filter which uses a low order Kalman filter to provide high accuracy tracking of nearly constant velocity targets, and switches to a higher order filter once the maneuver is detected.
- Maneuver detection is also used in an adaptive Kalman filter to switch to a higher level of process noise during a maneuver.

Maneuver Detection

- Maneuver detection can be formulated as a hypothesis testing problem and implemented by likelihood ratio test (LRT) based on the *Kalman filter innovations*.
- The central idea is that the sequences of *Kalman filter innovations* are white Gaussian random variables for a correctly modeled system.
- The probability of the measurement sequence is then expressible solely in terms of the innovations and their covariances.
- The statistics of the *Kalman filter innovations* can therefore be checked to see if they are consistent with the hypothesized model of the target dynamics.

Maneuver Detection

- Likelihood ratio test (LRT) uses:
(i) a test statistic
(ii) a threshold for the test.

- If the *test statistic*, which is a function of the measurement data, exceeds the threshold, a maneuver is declared; otherwise no maneuver is declared.

Maneuver Detection

- Assuming that the probability distribution (of the test statistic) under the maneuver and non-maneuver hypotheses is known, fixing a value for the *probability of false alarm* P_{MFA} determines the threshold for the test. The *probability of maneuver detection* P_{MD} and can then be calculated for the chosen threshold.

Single Target tracking using single Model Approach

- The tracking of the *single target* using *single model* is based on the choice of a (best) model to describe the maneuvering target. The chosen model is assumed as the true mode and a single filter runs based on it. This approach has several obvious flaws.

- First, the estimation does not take into account a possible mismatch between the target mode and the filter model.

- Second, the choice of the model is made offline and the estimation errors are not taken into account, even though they are the best indicator of the correctness of the chosen model.

Single Target tracking using Multiple Model Approach

Introduction to Multiple Model algorithms

- The MM algorithms allow that more than one model can be used at a time to match the current target mode.

- Besides diminishing the probability of mode and model mismatch and using the estimation errors to output a better overall estimate, the MM algorithms greatest benefit comes when used to solve target motion uncertainty.

Introduction to Multiple Model algorithms

- The *basic idea* is:
- To assume a set of models as possible candidates of the true mode in effect at the time.
- Run a bank of elemental filters, each based on a unique model in the set.
- Generate the overall estimates by a process based on the results of these elemental filters.
- The model-set is designated by M and is composed of N models, i.e., $M = \{m_1, \ldots, m_N\}$.

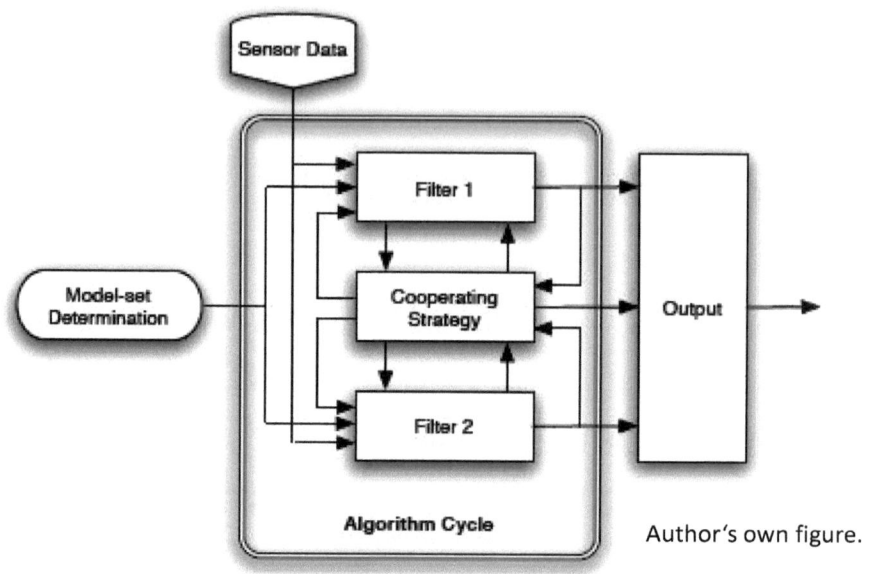

Author's own figure.

key components of MM estimation algorithms

1) Model-set determination:

- This includes both offline design and possibly online adaptation of the model set.

- A MM estimation algorithm uses a set of models, instead of a single model.

- The performance of a MM estimator depends largely on the set of models used.

- The major task in the application of MM estimation is the design (and possibly adaptation) of the set of multiple models.

key components of MM estimation algorithms

2) Cooperation strategy:

- This refers to all measures taken to deal with the discrete-valued uncertainties within the model set, particularly those for hypotheses about the model sequences.

- It includes not only pruning of unlikely model sequences, merging of 'similar' model sequences, and selection of (most) likely model sequences, but also iterative strategies, such as those based on the expectation-maximization algorithm.

key components of MM estimation algorithms

3) Conditional filtering:
This is the recursive estimation of the continuous-valued components of the hybrid process conditioned on some assumed mode sequence. It is conceptually the same as state estimation of a conventional system with only continuous-valued state.

4) Output processing:
This is the process that generates overall estimates using results of all filters as well as measurements. It includes fusing/combining estimates from all filters and selecting the best ones.

MM estimation algorithms

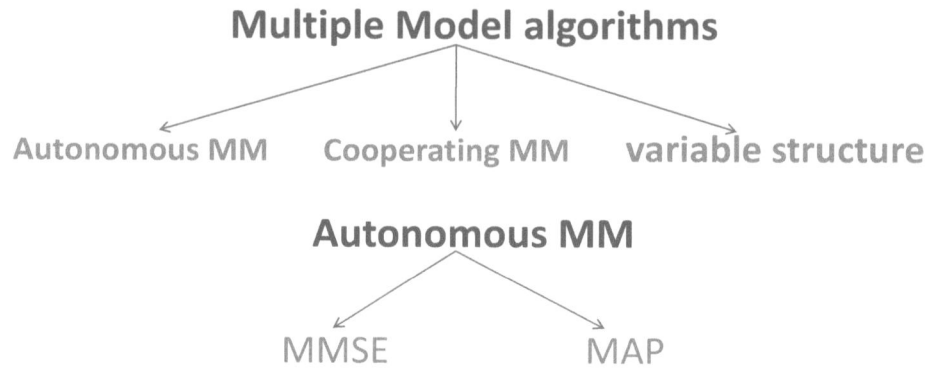

Multiple Model algorithms

Autonomous MM   Cooperating MM   variable structure

Autonomous MM

MMSE   MAP

Cooperating MM

• **The Interacting Multiple Model algorithm**

i.   Two-Stage Kalman Filter

Autonomous Multiple Model

- The *first generation* is characterized by the fact that each of its elemental filters operates *individually* and *independently* of all the other elemental filters.

- Its advantage over many non-MM approaches is due to its superior output processing of results from elemental filters to generate the overall estimate.

Autonomous Multiple Model

- The first generation of MM algorithms has _two_ main assumptions:

A_1. The true mode s is time invariant

$$(s_k = s, \ \forall k \ );$$

A_2. The true mode s at any time has a mode space S that is time invariant and identical to the time invariant finite model set M used (S_k = M, $\forall k$).

One Cycle of MMSE-AMM Algorithm

1. Model-conditioned filtering ($\forall m_i \in \mathbb{M}$) :

   Predicted state: $\hat{x}_{k|k-1}^{(i)} = F_{k-1}^{(i)} \hat{x}_{k-1|k-1}^{(i)}$

   Predicted covariance: $P_{k|k-1}^{(i)} = F_{k-1}^{(i)} P_{k-1|k-1}^{(i)} (F_{k-1}^{(i)})' + Q_{k-1}^{(i)}$

   Measurement residual: $\tilde{z}_k^{(i)} = z_k - H_k^{(i)} \hat{x}_{k|k-1}^{(i)}$

   Residual covariance: $S_k^{(i)} = H_k^{(i)} P_{k|k-1}^{(i)} (H_k^{(i)})' + R_k^{(i)}$

   Filter gain: $K_k^{(i)} = P_{k|k-1}^{(i)} (H_k^{(i)})' (S_k^{(i)})^{-1}$

   Update state: $\hat{x}_{k|k}^{(i)} = \hat{x}_{k|k-1}^{(i)} + K_k^{(i)} \tilde{z}_k^{(i)}$

   Update covariance: $P_{k|k}^{(i)} = P_{k|k-1}^{(i)} - K_k^{(i)} S_k^{(i)} (K_k^{(i)})'$

2. Model probability update ($\forall m_i \in \mathbb{M}$) :

   Model likelihood: $L_k^{(i)} \stackrel{assume}{=} \mathcal{N}(\tilde{z}_k^{(i)}; 0, S_k^{(i)})$

   Model probability: $\mu_k^{(i)} = \dfrac{\mu_{k-1}^{(i)} L_k^{(i)}}{\sum_j \mu_{k-1}^{(j)} L_k^{(j)}}$

3. Estimate fusion:

   Overall estimate: $\hat{x}_{k|k} = \sum_i \hat{x}_{k|k}^{(i)} \mu_k^{(i)}$

   Overall covariance: $P_{k|k} = \sum_i [P_{k|k}^{(i)} + (\hat{x}_{k|k} - \hat{x}_{k|k}^{(i)})(\hat{x}_{k|k} - \hat{x}_{k|k}^{(i)})'] \mu_k^{(i)}$

General structure of MMSE-AMM estimation algorithm with two model based filters

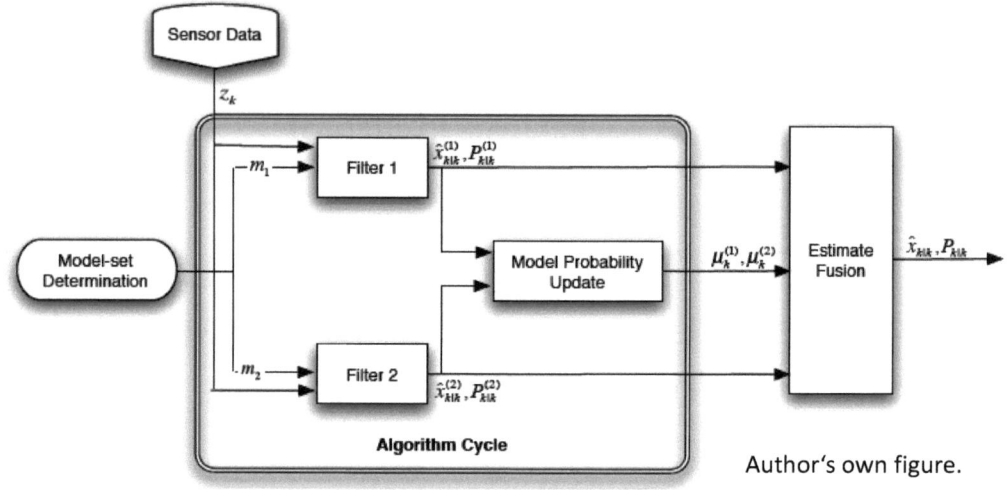

Author's own figure.

MMSE-AMM algorithm

- The design parameters of the MMSE-AMM and of the KF parameters are alike, except for the model set definition in contrast to a single model definition.

The MMSE-AMM design parameters are:

- The model set M structure.
- The system and measurement noises covariances (Q and R respectively).
- The initial state $\hat{x}_{0/0}$ and state covariance $P_{0/0}$.

Cooperating Multiple Model

- The second generation of MM algorithms inherits the first generation superior output processing and introduces the internal cooperation between elemental filters. Rather than keeping the filters working independently, this generation brings in the filter re-initialization, where all the outputs of the filters from the previous cycle are used in the current cycle to achieve a better performance.

Cooperating Multiple Model

- This generation relaxes the first generation assumptions:

A1'. The true mode sequence {s_k} is Markov, i.e., the mode evolves accordingly to the memoryless random process described by:

$$P\{s_{k+1}^{(j)}|s_k^{(i)}\} = \pi_{ij,k} \ \forall i,j;$$

A2'. The true mode s at any time has a mode space S that is time invariant and identical to the time-invariant finite model set M used (i.e., $S_k = M, \forall k$).

Cooperating Multiple Model

- A new variable is introduced to account the model history or model sequence

$$m^{k,l} = \{m^{(i_1,l)}, \ldots, m^{(i_k,l)}\}, \quad l = 1, \ldots, (N)^k$$

Where $i_{k,l}$ is the model index at time k from history l and

$$1 \leq i_{k,l} \leq N \; \forall k.$$

The Interacting Multiple Model algorithm

- The IMM estimator was originally proposed by Bloom.
- It is one of the most cost-effective classes of estimators for a single maneuvering target.
- The IMM has been receiving special attention in the last few years, due to its capability of being combined with other algorithms to resolve the multiple targets tracking problem.

The Interacting Multiple Model algorithm

- The sequence of events consisting of the true target mode sequence,

$$s^k = \{s_1, \ldots, s_k\},$$

- And the correspondent matching models sequence,

$$m^{(i^k)} = \{m^{(i_1)}, \ldots, m^{(i_k)}\},$$

The Interacting Multiple Model algorithm

- The IMM design parameters, which are once again the key to the algorithm performance, are:

- The model set M structure.

- The system and measurement noises covariances (Q and R respectively).

- The initial state $\hat{x}_{0/0}$ and state covariance $P_{0/0}$.

- The jump structure (usually Markov) and the transition probability π_{ji} between the models from the selected set.

The Interacting Multiple Model algorithm

- One of the main drawbacks of the first generation MM algorithms is its inability to handle mode jumps because each elemental filter is not aware of the overall estimate.

The IMM enables mode jumps in **_two ways_**:

- By re-initialization of the filters, each elemental filter computes estimates based on the overall estimate making the residuals smaller and facilitating mode jumps.

- By introducing a transition probability π_{ji}, which facilitates specific mode jumps, a priori considered to be more likely.

One Cycle of IMM Algorithm

1. Model-conditioned reinitialization ($\forall m_i \in \mathbf{M}$) :

   Predicted model probability: $\mu_{k|k-1}^{(i)} = \sum_j \pi_{ji} \mu_{k-1}^{(j)}$

   Mixing probabilities: $\mu_{k-1}^{j|i} = \pi_{ji} \mu_{k-1}^{(j)} / \mu_{k|k-1}^{(i)}$

   Mixing estimate: $\bar{x}_{k-1|k-1}^{(i)} = \sum_j \hat{x}_{k-1|k-1}^{(j)} \mu_{k-1}^{j|i}$

   Mixing covariance: $P_{k-1|k-1}^{(i)} = \sum_j [P_{k-1|k-1}^{(j)} + (\bar{x}_{k-1|k-1}^{(i)} - \hat{x}_{k-1|k-1}^{(j)})(\bar{x}_{k-1|k-1}^{(i)} - \hat{x}_{k-1|k-1}^{(j)})'] \mu_{k-1}^{j|i}$

2. Model-conditioned filtering ($\forall m_i \in \mathbf{M}$) :

   Predicted state: $\hat{x}_{k|k-1}^{(i)} = F_{k-1}^{(i)} \bar{x}_{k-1|k-1}^{(i)}$

   Predicted covariance: $P_{k|k-1}^{(i)} = F_{k-1}^{(i)} P_{k-1|k-1}^{(i)} (F_{k-1}^{(i)})' + Q_{k-1}^{(i)}$

   Measurement residual: $\tilde{z}_k^{(i)} = z_k - H_k^{(i)} \hat{x}_{k|k-1}^{(i)}$

   Residual covariance: $S_k^{(i)} = H_k^{(i)} P_{k|k-1}^{(i)} (H_k^{(i)})' + R_k^{(i)}$

   Filter gain: $K_k^{(i)} = P_{k|k-1}^{(i)} (H_k^{(i)})' (S_k^{(i)})^{-1}$

   Update state: $\hat{x}_{k|k}^{(i)} = \hat{x}_{k|k-1}^{(i)} + K_k^{(i)} \tilde{z}_k^{(i)}$

   Update covariance: $P_{k|k}^{(i)} = P_{k|k-1}^{(i)} - K_k^{(i)} S_k^{(i)} (K_k^{(i)})'$

3. Model probability update ($\forall m_i m_i \in \mathbf{M}$) :

   Model likelihood: $L_k^{(i)} \overset{assume}{=} \mathcal{N}(\tilde{z}_k^{(i)}; 0, S_k^{(i)})$

   Model probability: $\mu_k^{(i)} = \frac{\mu_{k|k-1}^{(i)} L_k^{(i)}}{\sum_j \mu_{k|k-1}^{(j)} L_k^{(j)}}$

4. Estimate fusion:

   Overall estimate: $\hat{x}_{k|k} = \sum_i \hat{x}_{k|k}^{(i)} \mu_k^{(i)}$

   Overall covariance: $P_{k|k} = \sum_i [P_{k|k}^{(i)} + (\hat{x}_{k|k} - \hat{x}_{k|k}^{(i)})(\hat{x}_{k|k} - \hat{x}_{k|k}^{(i)})'] \mu_k^{(i)}$

General structure of IMM estimation algorithm with two model based filters

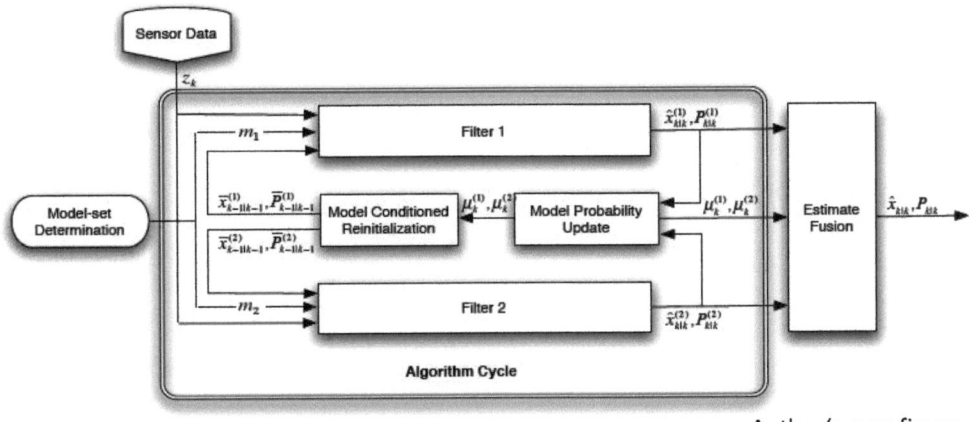

Author's own figure.

Multiple Target Tracking

- The Multiple Target Tracking (MTT) problem extends the single target tracking to a situation where the number of targets may not be known and can also be variable with time.

- Moreover, the measurements obtained are also not known, since they can be originated from any of the targets.

Multiple Target Tracking

- False alarms or measurements originated from clutter are an extra source of complexity in realistic applications.

- Thus, tracking multiple maneuvering targets is much more difficult than tracking a single maneuvering target since there is a challenge in correctly associating the measurements with the targets.

Problems of MTT

- **Single Target Tracking (STT):** addresses the problem of tracking a single target.

- **Data association (DA):** usually consists in ensuring that the correct measurement is given to each STT tracker so that the trajectories of each target can be accurately estimated.

The IMM-JPDAF design parameters are:

- The number of targets T.
- The model set M structure of each target r = 1, ... , T.
- The system and measurement noises covariances (Q and R respectively) of each target r = 1, ... , T.
- The initial state $\hat{x}_{0/0}$ and state covariance $P_{0/0}$ of each target r =1, ... , T.

- The jump structure (usually Markov) and the transition probability π_{ji} between the models from the selected set of each target r =1, ... , T.
- The probability of detection P_D^r of each target r =1, ... , T.
- The validation gate threshold.

For all targets r, ($r \in \{1 \dots T\}$):

1. Model-conditioned reinitialization ($\forall m_i \in \mathbb{M}$) :

   Predicted model probability: $\mu_{k|k-1}^{(i),(r)} = \sum_j \pi_{ji}^{(r)} \mu_{k-1}^{(j),(r)}$

   Mixing probabilities: $\mu_{k-1}^{j|i,(r)} = \pi_{ji}^{(r)} \mu_{k-1}^{(j),(r)} / \mu_{k|k-1}^{(i),(r)}$

   Mixing estimate: $\bar{x}_{k-1|k-1}^{(i),(r)} = \sum_j \hat{x}_{k-1|k-1}^{(j),(r)} \mu_{k-1}^{j|i,(r)}$

   Mixing covariance: $\bar{P}_{k-1|k-1}^{(i),(r)} = \sum_j [P_{k-1|k-1}^{(j),(r)} + (\bar{x}_{k-1|k-1}^{(r)} - \hat{x}_{k-1|k-1}^{(j),(r)})(\bar{x}_{k-1|k-1}^{(i),(r)} - \hat{x}_{k-1|k-1}^{(j),(r)})'] \mu_{k-1}^{j|i,(r)}$

2. Model-conditioned joint probabilistic data association filtering ($\forall m_i \in \mathbb{M}$ and $j = \{1, \dots, n_k\}$) :

   Predicted state: $\hat{x}_{k|k-1}^{(i),(r)} = F_{k-1}^{(i)} \bar{x}_{k-1|k-1}^{(i),(r)}$

   Predicted covariance: $P_{k|k-1}^{(i),(r)} = F_{k-1}^{(i)} \bar{P}_{k-1|k-1}^{(i),(r)} (F_{k-1}^{(i)})' + Q_{k-1}^{(i)}$

   Measurement validation: Find $y_k^{(j)} \in G_k(r)$

   Association probability: $\beta_{jr} = \sum_{\Theta} P\{\Theta|z^k\} \hat{\omega}_{jr}[\Theta]$

   Measurement residual: $\tilde{z}_k^{(ji),(r)} = y_k^{(j)} - H_k^{(i)} \hat{x}_{k|k-1}^{(i),(r)}$

   Weighted measurement residual: $\tilde{z}_k^{(i),(r)} = \sum_{j=1}^{n_k} \beta_{jr} \tilde{z}_k^{(ji)}(r)$

   Residual covariance: $S_k^{(i)} = H_k^{(i)} P_{k|k-1}^{(i),(r)} (H_k^{(i)})' + R_k^{(i)}$

   Filter gain: $K_k^{(i),(r)} = P_{k|k-1}^{(i)}(r) (H_k^{(i)})' (S_k^{(i),(r)})^{-1}$

   Update state: $x_{k|k}^{(i),(r)} = x_{k|k-1}^{(i),(r)} + K_k^{(i),(r)} \tilde{z}_k^{(i),(r)}$

   Update covariance: $P_{k|k}^{(i),(r)} = P_{k|k-1}^{(i),(r)} - (\sum_{j=1}^{n_k} \beta_{jr}) K_k^{(i),(r)} S_k^{(i),(r)} (K_k^{(i),(r)})' + K_k^{(i),(r)} [\sum_{j=1}^{n_k} \beta_{jr} \tilde{z}_k^{(ji),(r)} (\tilde{z}_k^{(ji),(r)})' - \tilde{z}_k^{(i),(r)} (\tilde{z}_k^{(i),(r)})'] (K_k^{(i),(r)})'$

3. Model probability update ($\forall m_i \in \mathbb{M}$) :

   Model likelihood: $L_k^{(i),(r)} \overset{assume}{=} \mathcal{N}(\tilde{z}_k^{(i),(r)}; 0, S_k^{(i),(r)})$

   Model probability: $\mu_k^{(i),(r)} = \frac{\mu_{k|k-1}^{(i),(r)} L_k^{(i),(r)}}{\sum_j \mu_{k|k-1}^{(j),(r)} L_k^{(j),(r)}}$

4. Estimate fusion:

   Overall estimate: $\hat{x}_{k|k}^{(r)} = \sum_i \tilde{x}_{k|k}^{(i),(r)} \mu_k^{(i),(r)}$

   Overall covariance: $P_{k|k}^{(r)} = \sum_i [P_{k|k}^{(i),(r)} + (\hat{x}_{k|k}^{(r)} - \hat{x}_{k|k}^{(i),(r)})(\hat{x}_{k|k}^{(r)} - \hat{x}_{k|k}^{(i),(r)})'] \mu_k^{(i),(r)}$

One Cycle of IMM-JPDAF Algorithm

References (1)

[1] X. Rong Li_ and Vesselin P. Jilkov, " A Survey of Maneuvering Target Tracking: Dynamic Models", SPIE Conference on Signal and Data Processing of Small Targets, Orlando, FL, USA, April 2000. (4048-22).

[2] Changzhen Qiu*, Zhiyong Zhang, Huanzhang Lu, and Huiwu Luo, "A Survey of Motion-Based Multitarget Tracking Methods", *Progress In Electromagnetics Research B, Vol. 62, 195–223, 2015.*

[3] Michael Beard, Ba-Tuong Vo, and Ba-Ngu Vo, "Bayesian Multi-target Tracking with Merged Measurements Using Labelled Random Finite Sets", IEEE TRANSACTIONS ON SIGNAL PROCESSING, VOL. 63, NO. 6, PP. 1433-1447, MARCH 2015.

[4] A. Dias, J. Capitan, L. Merino, J. Almeida, P. Lima and E. Silva, "Decentralized Target Tracking based on Multi-Robot Cooperative Triangulation", 2015 IEEE International Conference on Robotics and Automation (ICRA) Washington State Convention Center Seattle, Washington, May 26-30, 2015.

References (2)

[5] Graham W. Pulford, "A Survey of Manoeuvring Target Tracking Methods", arXiv:1503.07828v1[cs.SY] 6 Mar 2015.

[6] Jianfeng Wu, Shucai Huang, Guangjun He and Hongxia Kang, "H Filter and IMM Algorithm Applied On Target Tracking Problem ", International Journal of Control and Automation Vol.8, No.8 (2015), pp.297-308.

[7] Richard Altendorfer, "Observable dynamics and coordinate systems for automotive target tracking", arXiv:1005.3004v2 [cs.RO] 21 Sep 2014.

[8] Zheng Tang, Chao Sun, and Zongwei Liu, "The Tracking Algorithm for Maneuvering Target Based on Adaptive Kalman Filter", *The International Arab Journal of Information Technology, Vol. 10, No. 5, September 2013*

[9] Jon Ha Ryu, Du Hee Han, Kyun Kyung Lee, and Taek Lyul Song, "Prediction-based Interacting Multiple Model Estimation Algorithm for Target Tracking with Large Sampling Periods", International Journal of Control, Automation, and Systems, vol. 6, no. 1, pp. 44-53, February 2008.

References (3)

[10] X. Rong Li and Vesselin P. Jilkov," A Survey of Maneuvering Target Tracking—Part III: Measurement Models", Proceedings of SPIE Conference on Signal and Data Processing of Small Targets, San Diego, CA, USA, July-August 2001.

[11] Mohamad Hasan Bahari1, Ali Karsaz2 and Naser Pari, "HIGH MANEUVERING TARGET TRACKING USING A NOVEL HYBRID KALMAN FILTER-FUZZY LOGIC ARCHITECTURE", *International Journal of Innovative Computing, Information and Control* Volume 7, Number 2, February 2011.

[12] Kabita Hazra, B. N. Bhramar Ray, "Target Tracking in Wireless Sensor Network: A Survey", (IJCSIT) International Journal of Computer Science and Information Technologies, Vol. 6 (4) , 2015, 3720-3723

YOUR KNOWLEDGE HAS VALUE

- We will publish your bachelor's and
  master's thesis, essays and papers

- Your own eBook and book -
  sold worldwide in all relevant shops

- Earn money with each sale

Upload your text at www.GRIN.com
and publish for free